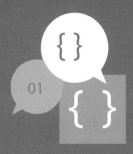

COMPUTING FOR KIDS

GW00579113

ROBOTS AND ARTIFICIAL INTELLIGENCE

NANCY DICKMANN

Gareth Stevens
PUBLISHING

1010101
10101

</>

Please visit our website, www.garethstevens.com.
For a free color catalog of all our high-quality books,
call toll free 1-800-542-2595 or fax 1-877-542-2596.

Cataloging-in-Publication Data

Names: Dickmann, Nancy.
Title: Robots and artificial intelligence / Nancy Dickmann.
Description: New York : Gareth Stevens Publishing, 2020. | Series: Computing for kids |
Includes glossary and index.
Identifiers: ISBN 9781538252642 (pbk.) | ISBN 9781538252659 (library bound)
Subjects: LCSH: Robots--Juvenile literature. | Robotics--Juvenile literature. |
Artificial intelligence--Juvenile literature.
Classification: LCC TJ211.2 D49 2020 | DDC 629.8'924--dc23

Published in 2020 by
Gareth Stevens Publishing
111 East 14th Street, Suite 349
New York, NY 10003

© 2020 BROWN BEAR BOOKS LTD

For Brown Bear Books Ltd:
Text and Editor: Nancy Dickmann
Children's Publisher: Anne O'Daly
Design Manager: Keith Davis
Designer and illustrator: Supriya Sahai
Picture Manager: Sophie Mortimer
Concept development: Square and Circus

CPSIA compliance information: Batch #CS20GS: For further information contact
Gareth Stevens, New York, New York at 1-800-542-2595.

Picture credits: Front Cover: Shutterstock;
Interior: iStock: 4kodiak 21, esp2k 11,
Maxiphoto 25, pat 22, VTT Studio 5; NASA:
7, 10; Shutterstock: Arica Studio 23, Antonio
Guillem 24, higyou 15, Mykola Holyatyak
12 intaratit 8, Jenson 4, Sergey Klopotov
26, Lopolo 20, Monkey Business Images
14, paparazza 17, piu piu 16, Scharfsinn
9, Song about summer 27, Sukpaiboon
13, WaveBreakMedia 18, Wellphoto 6,
Zapp2Photo 19.

Words in the glossary appear in bold type
the first time they are used in the text.

{ }

01

CONTENTS

WHAT IS A ROBOT?

There are robots at work in many factories.

There are robots in films. But are there robots in real life?

A robot is a special type of machine. People can **program** robots to do jobs. That means that robots can be given instructions. Then they follow the instructions to do a job. They can figure out what they need to do to get the job done.

Robots all around us

You may have already seen a robot in action! Robot vacuum cleaners clean the carpet. The self-checkout lane at the grocery store uses robots. Self-driving cars are a type of robot. There are even robotic toys that you can program yourself.

Japanese **engineers** have built robots that can chop vegetables and flip pancakes.

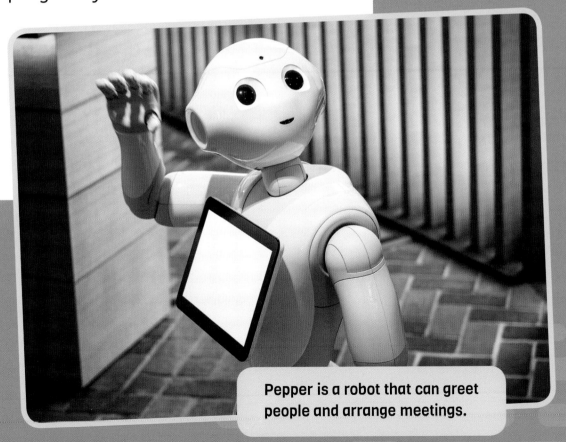

Pepper is a robot that can greet people and arrange meetings.

ROBOT JOBS

Robots are very good at some jobs. They are not so good at others!

Robots are not very good at writing stories or scoring goals. But they are great at doing simple, **repetitive** jobs. For example, a robot can tighten a screw on a new car. It can tighten screws all day without getting bored.

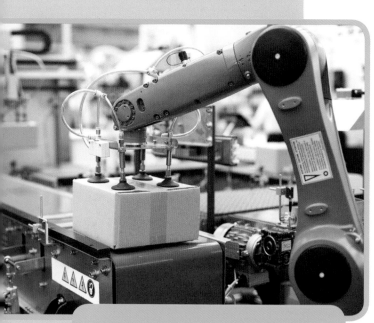

Robots can do the same job over and over without getting tired or making mistakes.

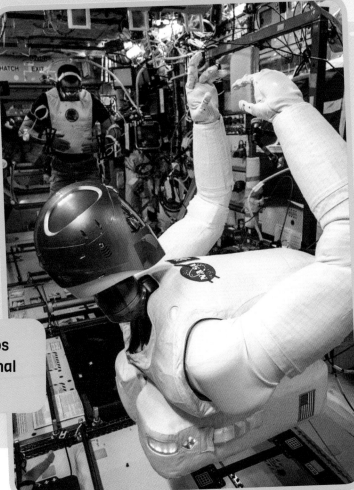

Robots can do dirty jobs, such as inspecting sewer pipes for leaks or blockages.

Robonaut is a robot that helps astronauts on the International Space Station.

Dangerous jobs

Some robots do jobs that are too dangerous for humans. They can travel deep in the ocean to find shipwrecks or other objects. They can go into a building where there may be a bomb.

SENSING

A robot is more complicated than a toaster. It can react to the world around it.

A robot is programmed to do a job. But to do it, it makes its own decisions. Those decisions are based on the information it takes in. A robot must be able to sense its environment.

You tell a remote-controlled car exactly where to go. It doesn't make its own decisions, so it isn't a robot.

Sensors

Robots have **sensors**. These are tools that can take in information about the surroundings. A camera is a type of sensor. There are also sensors that can sense light, temperature, **pressure**, or movement.

Some sensors use **laser** pulses to "see" objects that are near them.

Self-driving cars use sensors to follow road markings and keep a safe distance from other vehicles.

MAKING A PLAN

Once a robot has gathered information, its next job is to plan what to do.

Many robots have a computer inside that can process information. The computer takes in information from the robot's sensors. It uses this information to make a picture of the world around it.

A Mars **rover** has many different sensors. They all send information to its computer.

Running programs

A robot's computer figures out the best way to carry out its programmed task. If its sensors show that an object is in the way, it might change course to avoid it. If they show that it is getting too hot, it might switch on a fan.

Chess-playing robots can watch an opponent's move and then figure out the best response.

When a robot vacuum cleaner senses furniture in the way, it takes a new path.

TIME TO ACT!

Once a robot has a plan, it springs into action to carry it out.

Robots can act in many different ways. Some robots walk or roll on **tracks**. Others have arms with pincers for picking up objects. There are also robots that can climb or fly. A robot needs the right tools to do its programmed job.

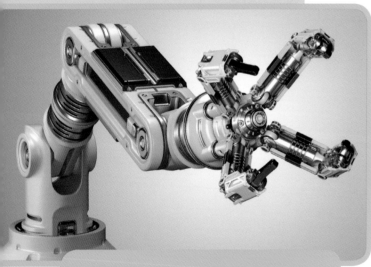

A factory robot doesn't need legs to carry out its program, just an arm to hold a tool.

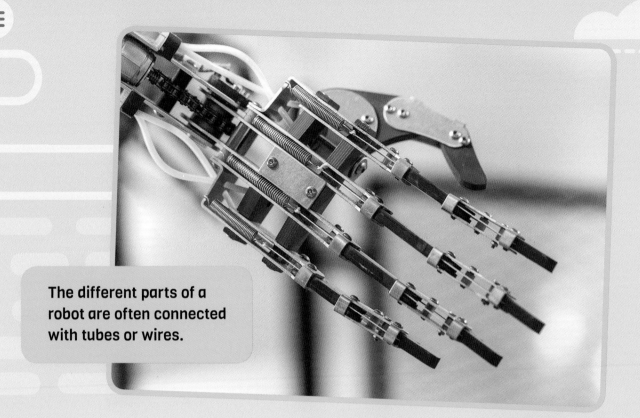

The different parts of a robot are often connected with tubes or wires.

Robot parts

Robots have mechanical parts that help them move. Many robots have motors and **pistons** that move in and out. They also have gears to adjust the way they move. Many robots are powered by batteries.

In some hospitals, a robot counts pills, puts them in bottles, and labels them for the patient.

ROBOTICS

It takes a lot of work to design and build a robot!

Robotics is a branch of technology. It is all about designing, building, and operating robots. Engineers need a lot of different skills to make a robot. They often work in teams. Each member tackles a different area.

Working in a team is a great way to share ideas about robots.

Building a robot

Robot designers think about what job they want the robot to do. They plan what it will look like. They add different types of sensors. They write a program for the robot to follow. Then they test the robot and think of ways to make it better.

Robotics engineers have designed robots that slither like snakes to get into tight spaces.

A robot called Big Dog has four legs and can carry heavy loads over rough ground.

HUMANOID ROBOTS

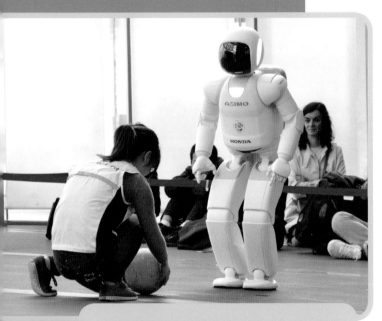

An android called Asimo can walk and even kick a soccer ball!

When most people think about robots, they probably think of one that looks like a person.

A robot that looks like a human is called an **android**. Some androids are only shaped like humans, with two legs and two arms. Other androids are covered with plastic "skin" to make them look like a real person.

How human?

Some people are more comfortable interacting with a robot that looks like a human. Other people find it creepy. But no matter how much an android looks like us, it is not human. It cannot love or have other emotions.

Building a robot that can walk on two legs is hard. It's easier to give the robot wheels!

It takes a lot of tiny motors to make a robot that can smile and frown like a person.

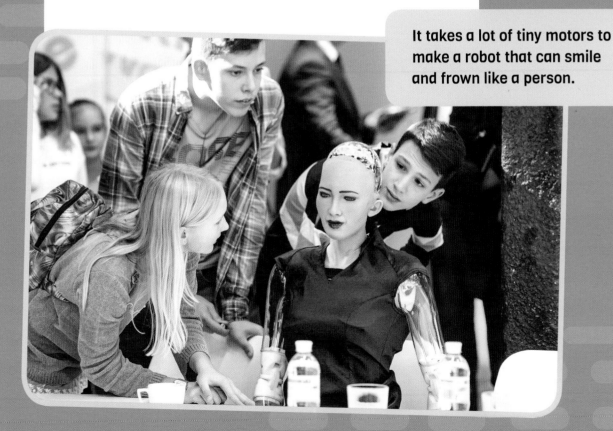

{ }

WHAT IS ARTIFICIAL INTELLIGENCE?

When you learn something new and remember it, you can apply that knowledge again.

Can a robot think and learn just like a human brain does?

Intelligence is the ability to think, learn, and solve problems. When a machine does this, it is called **artificial intelligence** (AI). A computer that can learn from experience is intelligent. A computer that just follows the same program over and over is not.

Using AI, robots can learn to identify people or objects.

Intelligent robots

Computers are really good at searching quickly through **data** and making calculations. Using AI, they can apply these skills to other areas. Some robots can recognize human faces or learn to play games such as chess.

Some newspapers have computers that use AI to write sports reports.

MACHINE LEARNING

You can figure some things out for yourself. Can a computer do the same thing?

When you learn, you take in facts. You listen and observe. Your brain makes connections between facts. It remembers them later. For example, if you try a new food and don't like it, your brain will remember next time you are offered it. It will remind you to say no.

Through experience, you learn how to move safely around a city.

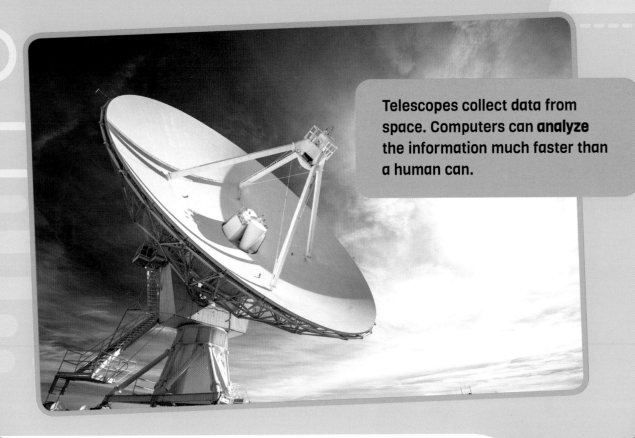

Telescopes collect data from space. Computers can **analyze** the information much faster than a human can.

Looking for patterns

Some computers learn in the same way. Programmers give them huge amounts of data, such as readings taken by telescopes looking at space. The computer can learn to look for patterns. The more it works, the better it gets. This is called **machine learning**.

Some of the most popular internet search engines are powered by machine learning.

VIRTUAL ASSISTANTS

You can ask your virtual assistant what the weather forecast is before you go out.

In some homes, you can turn on the lights or order groceries just by talking to a computer!

Have you ever used a virtual assistant? They are "smart speakers" that listen to your voice and carry out your **commands**. There are also virtual assistant programs on many smartphones. These devices are connected to the internet so they can look up information.

How they work

A virtual assistant can recognize human speech. It "wakes up" when you say a certain word. Then you can ask it to play music or add something to a shopping list. It can turn on the heating or look up a recipe.

Companies give virtual assistants names such as Siri or Alexa to make them seem more real.

A virtual assistant can connect to many different appliances, such as a television or stereo.

SMART DEVICES

A smart doorbell has a camera. It sends an image of the visitor to your phone.

It's not just robots and computers that can be "smart." **Appliances** also can be smart.

Smart devices are connected to the internet or a network in a household. You can control them using your voice or through a phone **app**. With smart devices, you can turn lights on and off or find out who's at the door, even if you're not at home.

A smart **thermostat** can save money and energy.

Keeping cool

A smart thermostat tracks your routines and your energy use. It automatically adjusts the temperature based on whether you're at home or whether you're asleep. It works out the best use of your heating and cooling system.

With a smart camera, you can use your phone to peek inside your fridge while you're at the grocery store!

TELLING THE DIFFERENCE

Engineers can build robots that act almost like humans. Could you tell the difference?

In an online chat, could you tell if the user chatting with you was a human or a robot? Computers are getting better at imitating real humans. These AIs use machine learning to learn how real people talk and react.

When you meet a robot face-to-face, it's easy to tell that it's not human.

The Turing Test

Alan Turing helped develop early computers. In 1950, he came up with a test that would tell if a computer could successfully imitate a human. There hasn't yet been a computer that scientists agree has passed the test. But they think it will happen soon.

Films show robots that fool people into thinking they're real. So far, these robots are only fiction.

When you chat online, it's harder to tell if it's a robot or a human.

CHATBOT 15:1
OK

QUIZ

Try this quiz and test your knowledge of robots and AI! The answers are on page 32.

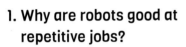

1. Why are robots good at repetitive jobs?

a. because they can learn from their mistakes

b. because they don't get tired or bored

c. because they're not very clever

2. Why isn't a remote-controlled car a robot?

a. because it doesn't make its own decisions

b. because it runs on batteries

c. because it doesn't have arms and legs

3. What do sensors do?

a. teach karate

b. build robots and other machines

c. take in information about the world around them

4. What does a robot's computer do?

a. takes in information and makes a plan

b. tries to act like a real human

c. helps you order a takeout

5. Why do some robots slither like snakes?

a. because it looks really cool

b. so that they can get into small spaces to do their job

c. because the designers forgot to add the legs

6. What is an android?

a. a type of tropical fish

b. a sensor that measures temperature

c. a robot that looks like a human

7. What is artificial intelligence?

a. a machine thinking and solving problems like a human brain does

b. a language for programming robots

c. pretending that you know what you're talking about when you actually don't have a clue

8. How can a computer pass the Turing Test?

a. by processing 1 million commands per second

b. by convincing a person that it's really a human

c. by keeping your home at a constant temperature

{ }

01

GLOSSARY

analyze to examine something in detail in order to find patterns or explain it

android a robot that looks like a human

app a computer program designed to do a particular job, usually on a smartphone or tablet

appliances household machines such as a toaster or a dishwasher

artificial intelligence computer systems that can do jobs that would normally require human intelligence

commands orders or instructions given to a computer

data information that is stored or used in a computer, in the form of a series of ones and zeroes

engineer a person who designs and builds things, such as robots

laser a beam of focused light that can be used to sense distance

machine learning the ability of a computer to learn from experience

piston part of a machine that moves up and down

pressure a pushing force

program to write a set of coded instructions for a computer to follow, or the set of coded instructions

repetitive doing the same thing over and over

rover a robotic vehicle that drives across the surface of a distant planet or moon

sensor a device that detects or measures something such as heat or light

thermostat a device that controls the temperature in a building by giving commands to the heating and cooling systems

tracks metal or rubber bands around the wheels of a heavy vehicle, such as a bulldozer, which allow it to move over rough ground

FIND OUT MORE

Books

Ives, Rob. *Build Your Own Robots (Makerspace Models)*. Minneapolis, Minn.: Hungry Tomato, 2018.

Leigh, Anna. *Cutting-Edge Artificial Intelligence (Searchlight Books)*. Minneapolis, Minn.: Lerner Publications, 2018.

Lepora, Nathan. *DKfindout! Robots*. New York: DK Children, 2018.

Swanson, Jennifer. *Everything Robotics: All the Photos, Facts, and Fun to Make You Race for Robots*. Washington, DC: National Geographic Kids, 2016.

Websites

Go here to find answers to questions about computers: **www.bbc.com/bitesize/subjects/zyhbwmn**

Learn more amazing facts about robots: **kids.kiddle.co/Robot**

Discover more about what robots can do: **idahoptv.org/sciencetrek/topics/robots/facts.cfm**

This website will tell you more about how robots work: **science.howstuffworks.com/robot.htm**

Want a simple explanation of AI? Try this website: **www.kidscodecs.com/what-is-artificial-intelligence**

INDEX

Quiz answers
1. b; 2. a; 3. c; 4. a; 5. b; 6. c; 7. a; 8. b